I0796244

Humanimus

Humanimus

Poems

David Huebert

Palimpsest Press
1171 Eastlawn Ave.
Windsor, Ontario. N8S 3J1
www.palimpsestpress.ca

Printed and bound in Canada
Cover design and book typography by Ellie Hastings
Edited by Jim Johnstone

Palimpsest Press would like to thank the Canada Council for the Arts and the Ontario Arts Council for their support of our publishing program. We also acknowledge the assistance of the Government of Ontario through the Ontario Book Publishing Tax Credit.

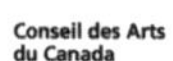

LIBRARY AND ARCHIVES CANADA CATALOGUING IN PUBLICATION

TITLE: Humanimus : poems / David Huebert.
NAMES: Huebert, David, author.
IDENTIFIERS: Canadiana (print) 20200278657
Canadiana (ebook) 20200278681

ISBN 9781989287569 (SOFTCOVER) | ISBN 9781989287576 (EPUB)
ISBN 9781989287583 (KINDLE) | ISBN 9781989287590 (PDF)

CLASSIFICATION: LCC PS8615.U3 H86 2020 | DDC C811/.6—DC23

Table of Contents

Humanimus

Bite Song

Oil Weather

Phonemevolution

for Rose & Sybille

"... we are dealing with a humanimalchine."

—Dominic Pettman

Humanimus

The Call

An ocean, aflame
under metabolic night.

A phone rings
in The Faraway.

This is the call
you have been waiting for.

Sleep gentle, gentle.
Out of batteries.

The water burns,
the sockets bleed

voltaic seas:
amperes, empires, hertz.

Mutants' Songnet

"The weight of future oceans,
glowing and nearly empty,
each lowly mutant

lowing for a mate."

—Catriona Wright

We fell in love in the tailing pond
where you'd built your shopping cart hutch.
The sky was a rerun—
canned laughter, technocolor gore.
You fed me nitrogen-rich popcorn,
brandished your acetate tongue.
Sucking your fingers, you asked if I, too, loved
to loathe the tang of ethanol.
First base was a gas pump—weep, seep, dry.
We mated in microwaves,
watched our brood slime around the block.
I'm sorry it had to end, and I'm sorry you cried.
But I needed to see rainbows dance
in your crocodile tears, petroleum eyes.

Selfie

Atatürk statues groan *merhaba,*
broccoli blooms in red earth. Are you
Turkish? Am I German? Our ankles chapped
with fungus or bug bites. Diarrhea—

you blamed the fruit, the volunteer harem
at the Ecofarm, the handsome owner
insisting: this is not Asia. Her name:
Celine? Camille? Pretty name, someone said.

She said make sure to close the door because
rats. The fish, educating your legs in
Turgutreis, the gout-swollen man
at the Lycian tombs, milking liras from chapped

tourist teats, a democracy of hawkers
chanting selfie selfie selfie. Conjure
a place where saying thank you requires
six syllables. Requires six syllables.

Paradise: the sun's drunk diaspora
over Kuşadasi—smeared yolk hazing
Antalya, Çanakkale, Istanbul,
these heavens eclipsed by failed uploads, smeared

index rinds. Walking lonely trails through tanned
mountains, new words sand our beige and peeling
tongues: *Koftë, iki, alasmaladuch.*
Here, in the land of beautiful horses,

the land of rooftop terraces, the world
that never rains, a gravedigger squats
under elderberry leaves and points his hose
at me. Paradise: bus cushions frothing

with sweat, monuments holding duck
face, ochre smeared on church ceilings.
Paradise is never watching
another sunset without selfie stick in hand.

Cube Root Hand

after Stelarc's "Third Hand"

The Third Hand was weary of shaking its fist,
longed to complete a high five.
Once the last human arm had rotted,
the Third Hand broke away, bored deep
into the sand, drilled past the shale
and limestone, pried a spring of sable fluid,
floated infantile through amniotic dark.

Centuries winked before the Third Hand
emerged, bamboozled Gravity, thumbed
the cavities of a ruptured sky.
The Third Hand watched *Terminator 2*
until it fell through a time travel paradox,
looked out across the barren dessert
and whispered *hasta la vista, vista.*

The Third Hand cackled backward down
double-helix waterslides, waddled through
liquid nitro superstorms, wept lube into
the shattered fragments of its frozen thumb.
Alit on the ground and found itself still
walking, a song without a throat.
The Third Hand asked its pony, Epiphone:
was it also the First Hand, and the Last?

Moonrise

Burn enough hectares and the day scars black,
blossoms into cornflowers as you tread

plastic bottles, gulp the last acid wave.
A Chinese lantern floats—glowing, lovely,

scorched.
A methane rose, abloom.

The bruised moon will sulk a googol of lifespans,
sass its kimono open: fuchsia, lavender, tangerine.

Closeted

Your closet is the same size as mine,
which neither of us thinks is fair.
The cat reposes in yours, shed fur
turning that black backpack
into a hairy critter. Knapsacklesloth.

Mine holds hockey skates,
drying from last night's shinny.
You don't like the smell.
But this isn't about my feet—
it's about your closet, our cat.

What I'm trying to say is something
about the feel of your kimono, how
it only excites me when your skin's
underneath. The strings of your
dresses dangle, little girl legs

on buses, and the cat swats.
No doubt I'm projecting (the right
word must start with anthropo)
but I insist she paws those dangly
bits because she misses you.

What I'm trying to say has something
to do with the way your closet looks
the same when you're not here—
how that's scary and comforting,
how I went in there for the first time

and just sniffed, conjuring the chimp
in me to smell the bonobo in you.
How maybe that was weird
but at least I didn't try on your clothes.
Or did I? Would you mind?

Miss Trans-Canada

Parliaments of bottlenecks,
Silverado referendums,
pipelines clenched with hemorrhoids,
beavers gnawing the last maple, damming
rivers with Q-tips, tampons, tar.

And Miss Trans-Canada,
concrete Aphrodite, one fin in
Victoria, one in Haida Gwaii,
long tail spanning prairies,
buttocks cupping little London,
Maritime cleavage softening
Newfoundland's Roman nose.

Watch this road-stitched beauty
stand and start to flop,
towns clinging helpless as
kelp on Poseidon's back,
Neons and Escalades cartwheeling
down mountains, skipping over lakes.

Cringe as she remembers
the Frankensteins that made her,
shudder while she recalls a time
before we sewed the rivers shut,
when roads were made of water.

Trichotillomaniac Reports from Periscope Depth

"I looked for the head of Mr. Apollinax rolling under a chair
Or grinning over a screen
With seaweed in its hair.
I heard the beat of centaur's hoofs over the hard turf"

—T.S. Eliot

Begin with the submarines lurking in the harbour—
fingers twitching, spurring, newly ravenous for hair.
Sea wolves gasping for a path between the mines,
digits trotting scalp for strands to clutch and pry.
Did I leave blood-darkened tufts in colleagues' mailboxes?
Did I request my wife to sew a merkin from the chaff,
beg her to wear that patchy beard about her wax-bright loin?
Did I dream my brain had been pushed through colanders,
dried into nests of spaghetti? Did I pine my pate a barren earth?
I heard the beat of centaur's hoofs over the hard turf.

It began with the submarines lapping at the coping
of the continental shelf. The harbour only so deep
and a homing finger revealing a metastasis of mines.
Whispers of sea wolves turning serpent, weaving watery dreams.
A convoy waiting to embark when the U-boat surfaced,
taunting nudity of its slick black curvature leaving
plum-cheeked lads aghast. Lads due for Normandy
and my hands climbing ears, longing for a single grey lovely.
I took to sitting in front of mirrors, scalp scabbed and bare,
I looked for the head of Mr. Apollinax rolling under a chair.

You see it was the submarines. The bloody submarines.
It was centaur's hooves hoovering, thirsty centaurs galumphing
through deserts where tanks pivoted, parched for gas.
It was a smiling head rolling through the library.
It was convoys of tooth-broke boys.
It was cystic pebbles in skinned knees. Oil wells smouldering
in the gulf. It was a carnival of wifely privates,
a bearded lady's come-hither sneer. It was the autopsy,
black fluid drooling viscous from veins.
It was a head coated in plasticine, grin gasped in a synthome of screens.

It ended, I'll have you know, with the submarines.
Believe it ended with diesel-electric submarines.
By then my scalp was flecked with gore.
By then my scalp was a herpic hinterland and still my claws
crawled the scree of chap. My fingers ravenous eagles,
my mind a ravaged Prometheus, and then I submerged, went underway,
swashed about at periscope depth and then deeper,
out past the Sable Gully, over the Grand Banks into the Sohm.
I bobbed across the ocean floor, saw the creature emerge:
a one-eyed damsel, her hair seaweed forests, a luff in a breeze of sea.

Reclining Universe

after Marc Bolan

You've got the universe reclining
in your hair while your Jaguar slinks
up hairpin mountain roads, the bald shepherd waving
from the valley as you soar off the cusp.

Once you lay belly-up in the lake, hair fanned
and rippling in a kelp aurora. In the forest a hare
darted from the beast with hairy tongues, demons
revved harelip chariots but you were oblivious
in the cool water remembering Harry the Hare Krishna
and the girl with the sunset lips, her hair a boreal fishtail.

All of this melting to marrow in your mind's hairline
fracture. How harebrained that it ends here—
the road's hair split to frizz as you soar blue skies
humming a comb through your hair.

Cithaeron

His parents have left him
to the brute wind, skittering
night. Bats flit and dive
through red-eyed dark,
his hunger squirming in a fist of thirst.

One day they will call him
Swollen Foot, Puzzle Solver,
Plague Ender. One day they
will call him Father Killer,
Sister Father, Mother Lover.

Mad with need-to-know,
he will rage against his allies,
bite the chafed nipple of Fate.
His daughters will recall two
raw sockets, rank pits of gore.

Climbing towards this child,
does the shepherd know the plot?
Boy meets oracle, flees to Thebes,
leaves father at crossroads,
nostrils clotted with gnats.

Yes, he cries. I know it all.
Still, he breaks the boy's shackles,
hands him a biscuit and flask.
Guiding the child down the slope,
he moans, What else can we do?

Zelda

I was dreaming Paris, a *musician ambulant* plucking pizzicato,
dreaming swans on the Seine, teaching their young to fly.
The river was Tiber, was Thames, was Wimahl
and I was a canoe let loose, a Kalamata drifting
martini, approaching the fierce liquid
tongue between the rocks, my body Oblivion's siren
riding astonished through the dip and gliding on—

I'd been treading this liquid dream for eighteen years,
was not ready for smoke to curl up from the dumbwaiter,
for the screams of all those women with wrists tied to beds,
the alchemy of lungs transposing breath into sky,
watching black-magic carpets ride this sabretooth
sorceress night. Air thickening and the blackened faces
wailing, rasping, coarse sheets eager handmaids to
the crackling hissing rising walls that enclosed
these writhing creatures, their screams racing up and up
until they made abyss of this warped world.

When the smoke began to clot my lungs and I could taste
the ash on my teeth, I dreamt my screaming breath a swan,
flapping rabid before rising gentle over the vast purple
lawns of North Carolina. One of it's young flew
alongside or was that its mate or former self or did it matter
as two swans flew away together from an asylum in flames.
I was dreaming Paris, dreaming Seine, diving into its cool,
kicking my mermaid's tail and launching down,
down and up, somehow, at once. I was a boomerang
arcing sidelong, coiling skyward, and no hand, no ground,
no hand or ground or gravity ever again would catch me.

Therese

"Beethoven would have been astounded and probably outraged to know that eventually this little courtship item became one of the most famous things he ever wrote."

—Jan Swafford

A tremor in the loins of the earth—thump of war and bleat of love, blunt indices of anguish and triumph and the man palming floorboards as if to read you through a braille of splinters. Groping rendered oak as if to tease your anima and curl it into arpeggios, into thirty-second notes, into bagatelle. Vienna a thunder he cannot hear as you lie on the divan playing Schnapsen with Anna, the first blast ruddering your home and François your tutor, François your lover, François calling from the library and out of the debris this aging peasant holding a note, fondling a tune.

Napoleon writes to his lover, requesting that she not bathe until his return.

Your sister is to be a baroness and your father telling this mad-eyed jester with grey shrubs in his nose that even if you loved him, it could not be done. The mortars and howitzers arcing over the Danube and this rheumatic conjurer unable to listen, kneeling in his quarters striving to unravel the knots of age and class, churn iron into silk.

The conqueror rides through the city gates, Marengo placing his hooves delicately so as not to disturb the undergrowth of corpses.

A scavenger, a magician, a bard. Trying to wrest beauty from the wreckage and what he produces is this bagatelle in 3/8 time, left unpublished until after your death. Found among your personal papers long after the composer was dead—why did you keep the love song of the man you'd spurned?

J'arrive, he writes. *J'arrive.*

How many times you thought to burn that manuscript but the fact was you still liked to play, that each time you ran through the Poco moto and raced into the arpeggios you felt the past thrum through your fingers, saw your adolescence quiver like trees in a lake. The music quickening, panting, recalling the thrilling artillery and the searching shudder of François' lips and even if it was simple and over too fast you could imagine no lovelier coffin, no sweeter tomb.

Amalia

"Amalia Freud, his beautiful young mother, much closer to his age than Jacob Freud, his all too conquerable father, mysteriously disappears from Freud's mythologies of self and world."

—Maud Ellman

The refinery dazzles your window:
a crematory circus, a corona of gore,
a limping seducer, gilded teeth
unable to refresh a mammatus of rot.

From Danube to Black Sea
a pipeline sutures the cities
of your youth—Brody, Boryslaw, Odessa.
Fate's fossils melding in Freiburg

where you roamed the Schwarzwald,
marveled at the boy, that gash in the night,
a nebula leaking through your nipple
to greet the newborn's curious teeth.

Grey eyes crawled your body as he blinked
a century of oil, antiquities of thunder.
Nine years old and his scientist eyes
provoked a vague tickle, a mnemonics

of the womb—the rented room in the locksmith's
house and the boy born faceless,
head wrapped in slick hood, a flap like
lucent foreskin. You tugged it off to find him

screaming and hale, peeled that blank face
with slithering ease to greet your fearful
firstborn—how could you have known there
would be seven more? You hid that caul

to let it dry, kept it in the cellar with the teeth
he shucked and set on your pillow
like the limpid trophies of cats. Was it strange
that you took those teeth in your mouth,

let the saltmetal taste dream over your tongue
as your husband torqued the bed
and the boy looked on, storms curdling
in his grey eyes. The boy born in 1856,

named Sigismund, named Schlomo, the boy
you called goldener, Sigi, mein Sohn.
Three years later the world bloomed black—
Petrolia, Oil Creek, your girlhood Galicia.

Thirty-four years a widow in Vienna,
you never told the boy you'd returned
to the shtetl, walked the streets of Brody
and smelled that petrified plankton sear.

Was it strange that you longed, then,
to bring that time-dark ooze to your lips,
that you spent solitary nights picturing
each child afloat in an amnion of oil?

Not curious because you knew, had always
known—the boy would say *Todestreib*
and he would mean that demon fluid, mean
oil and blood and breastmilk and you,

eighty-five then, would feel that darkness
rise and whisper that your children—
Rosa and Mitzi, Pauli and Dolfi—
would go to Treblinka, to Theresienstadt,

that the oil would leak and burn through
Boryslaw, that the SS would pile
the intellectuals in the Jewish Cemetery,
and you would say no to the death drive.

Moon

Your glow no simulacrum of sun.
In you like heat in fire,
mind in brain, sickness in bloom.

Do you remember when the Colonizers
wiped their boots on you?
Do you recall your first penetration,

the unlubed flagpole fang?
None of this changes what you are:
lucid delirium, ecstatic melancholy, epiphanous oblivion.
White dressing in the sphincteral dark,

all space your blacklight.
And me, here. Breathing, balancing,
in the stark and glowing yard.
The stillness sways. You whisper back.
We glow through emotions.

Season's End

The snow, the way it is here in March:
exhaust-scorched, coarse with road salt.
The rust and the sleet, endless cloy of lines.

The snow, the way it was there in April,
afternoon haze and distance, distance, distance.
Below, the bootpack stitched seams of seasons.

You never knew why it was called "corn snow"
but you knew, gleefully, what it meant:
all things skimmed in steeped-gold glaze.

The snow did not come in February.
You'd near given up when the March sky bloated,
trees stooping in the wealth of new white coats.

On the way down: drunken twilight
and the wilting syrup sun. Charging
too fast but still so safe and free.

Near the bottom great gaps of exposed
rock and you had to leap over them,
sparks spattering the snow behind.

Even then you knew there could be no joy
commensurate. You did not know how long
you would struggle to never get it back.

Bite Song

Wild in Me

How to recall this wild in me?
My toes have forgotten how to grasp:
Atrophied feet push pedals, deaf
To strut of songs from time before.

My toes have forgotten how to grasp,
This mouthy mind won't let me hear
The strut of songs from time before,
When handsteps whispered, soft as rain.

This mouthy mind won't let me hear
The time before this motorroar,
When handsteps whispered soft as rain
(Each murmur hummed and purred in me).

The time before this motorroar:
Each blade of grass a lilting tongue,
Each murmur hummed and purred in me:
Each colour pealed, and death was young.

Each blade of grass a lilting tongue,
Teeth wandering from bite to song:
Each colour pealed, and death was young,
And life was heaving, mending, gone.

Atrophied feet push petals, deaf
And charging through explosive truth:
There's no such time as time before,
But I recalled this wild, this me.

Blades of Grass

All the blades of grass
were weeping under
a side-scroll Nintendo sky.

O, tonic dreamscape:
peach and rose,
palm-tree green,
synthetic strawberries
and bananas
jumping rainbows
in galactic vasts.

We dropped Wendy's
fries on the lawn
and all the grass-mouths
opened at once,

crooning *cumulus*,
howling *sodium*,
lilting chloride.

Someone passed a Frosty.
My tastebuds wailed
their single word:
saccharine.

Owl

Owl, with your wet-sand coat and your
slow black eyes, where is your parliament?

A frantic swell of harried caws,
I turn the corner to watch you leap

from the gaunt maple, spread your wings,
send fluttering the coal-black birds.

They swerve to nip your neck,
feathers blizzarding the clay-dark sky.

Wind creaks the woods, sunlight gasps
through meagre branches. You hobble close,

stroke my cheek, your wing a gnawed forgiveness.
You see me, know I'm tall and pale for a crow.

Tails

Your soundless shadow, fast and low,
diced umbra of my bicycle wheel.
Twinned fluttering disks of dark.

How time winces, watching
you alight on the lamppost,
adjust your tail. Not slower

but twisted, like a ribbon of rind
peeled off a lemon, like
cloying fingernail grins.

My mind becomes a ponytail.
When the owl attacked that jogger's
bobbing skull. At the farm four vultures

gliding, curiosities pert as follicles.
And of course the things we have
no longer we long to replace.

Lacking a Jar

Lumps in the grass, slurs of twilight
turning rabbit. Who can say
what moves in grassy underworlds,
how deep the homes of bees?

The first time she saw them
she darted, catlike and swiping.
Lacking a jar, she wanted nothing
but to take them in her hands.

Why do writhing lovers bend bedrooms
while here in open darkness
bats descend on the fireflies?
She is pawing, pawing the sky—
stars twitch like fleas in the fur of night.

Scorpions

O, full of scorpions is my mind, dear wife!
Scorpions scuttling Sonoran bathroom floors
while the radio blares the Scorpions,
scorpions rocking me like a hurricane while I dream
scorpions over the border talking about your mother's
scorpion tongue. She asked me my sign and
I said Scorpio, told her I scorched ions for a living
after which she showed me her scorpion tattoo
and the neon rainbow of scorpions in the bathtub,
scorpions teeming and telsoned, dear wife!
I held your new scorpion hand then, took your aculeus
in mine. Scorpions glowed metasomal
and venom zoomed through our scorpion tails,
eight scorpion legs seeking bathtubs to cool the mind.

Familiaris

> *"In 1692 nineteen men and women and two dogs were convicted and hanged for witchcraft in a small village in eastern Massachusetts."*
>
> —Cristopher Bigsby

Astride the mares on gobbling nights,
a sound to quake a steady bowel,
the whisper-lurk as darkling hounds
stalk corridors for sniffs of fowl.

Scarlet wiles, Antinomian wights,
strange nightmares tread this wilderness,
the whisper-wish of moonlit lakes
as überhounds make shadows prowl.

Wild hounds grow too familiar,
their bodies begging, *infiltrate.*
That lupine lilt, a beast possessed,
candles hissed through air befouled.

The dogs not hanged, the girls unhinged,
the blasts that stilled those lolling tongues—
the princess, in a castled mate,
conspired to end their frenzied howls.

The canine gore stains pillories
and spirits wail through skulking woods.
What witches lack familiars,
what spells astir in nesting owls?

Where are the graves, what record drawn,
what blushed apology for you?
Your whinge the ash of centuries,
a dying friend, a tender growl.

Granger

> *"There was a youth whose name was Thomas Granger... this year detected of buggery, and indicted for the same, with a mare, a cow, two goats, five sheep, two calves and a turkey. Horrible it is to mention, but the truth of the history requires it."*
>
> —William Bradford, 1642

> *"And if a man lie with a beast, he shall surely be put to death: and ye shall slay the beast."*
>
> —Leviticus 20.15

It was you who with your sallow root
had all but slain the animals.

Your lowered pants in winter chill:
they found it strange (the animals).

Steaming flesh, slithering pink,
were they in pain, the animals?

Your moon-white hams, your canid yips,
the brayed refrain of animals.

Not thief, perhaps, but borrower?
Your need was drained in animals.

What inklings gnawed your mind that night?
Were they deranged, the animals?

The sheep gave birth to biped lambs,
they burned with shame, the animals.

Human smiles in clouds of wool.
They ascertained, the animals.

The elders from the pillory:
"This man has maimed the animals."

You hung to let the others dream
their tables laid with animals.

Bears Once

> *"There is no record of a living bear of the grizzly species in California—the state whose emblem is the Great Golden Bear—since 1922."*
>
> —Bessie Doak Haynes and Edgar Haynes

Once there were bears in California,
the woods fat with their smell.
Once bears roamed among redwoods—
aged trees that wouldn't be felled.

Once there were bears whose longing
ruled the rivers, bears who roared
clouds into motion, bears whose sleep
was vast as the wants it quelled.

Once there were bears whose hunger
was the song the salmon danced to,
their churning scales gleaming
cosmic in the river's swell.

Once the bears made the moon grin,
made the ants howl, tore the sky to
ragged strips and drank its plasma—
rainbows poured from punctured shell.

Once there was gold in California,
gold and guns and mustangs galloping
mustangs galloping through the ages,
driving dust to stanch the maker's well.

Once there were tears in California,
tears that flowed from glaciers and
melted fourteen hydroelectric dams
into a single harried, desolate yell:

there were bears, once, in California.

Appaloosa

"The spotted horses had become so great a symbol of resistance that from then on the Army was under written orders to destroy every one that it came across, and in one instance, 400 head were driven into a canyon and shot."

—Elaine Walker

The sky a scowl of cloud and everything in you twitching to run. Your coat a blacklight galaxy on a cloudless prairie night, the swirl and zoom and deke of you distilled in the sear of an air burnt sour. Kin wailing and hoofs thundering, thundering off the rising walls. Gunshot boom and crack and you have never known how could you have known such underworldly clamour. How you trusted the men that bred you and the ones before. The man they called Tooyalaket, the man whose cause of death was recorded "heartbreak." The men who fed you and washed you and rode you through the bear's paw, rode you through gunshot and scream and you stayed brave as the bit in your mouth, fierce as the spurs in your flank. You did not know the why but you knew the need in those razor heels. Your love for your riders was a riddle of comfort and fear and you knew if you ran fast enough through the dread you would reach the other side. So you obeyed the ones that drove you here, into the barred teeth of the world, the air a sickness and all the wild that made you wanting nothing but to flee. The walls rising jagged and closing, closing, and you charging deeper always deeper because there's only ever one way through. All your ancestors screaming that this is the time to break and flee but the walls the walls and the horses shrieking and shrieking. Gunshots cracking and walls teetering and stepping on hooves then bodies, bodies, a waste of bodies, that thunder-crack of gunshot and you cannot hear where it is this stream of fallen lovers and mothers and kin and stepping on crushing a face and all the bodies so close and toppling until your leg snaps and the world teeters and warps and a strange release when you are down in the dirt at last, down in the dirt and dreaming of the day you ran fleet across the plains that named you. Salmon clotted thick in the river like a single writhing serpent. Herds of buffalo droning and you flying riderless, breaking untouchable through the time before the wildness was lost and your name is your being is a thrill is a song:

Appaloosa
Appaloosa
Appaloosa

County

I wouldn't trust a bovine prophet
but you say you'd take these motley oracles
over teleprompters and green screens,
you'd choose Herefords over weathermen
despite fluorescent teeth and cowboy tans.

Welcome to Bruce: enjoy beef everyday
and the fields green after rainless weeks.
Will we arrive to cows staggering on a Huron
drunk dry? The Mennonites buggying
along the shoulder, a chronospasm

glitching me back to Boryslaw, to Odessa,
to Waldheim. My grandmother's darkest secret:
watching *Jeopardy* every day of her life.
It will not rain and it will not rain and the sun
leaks over the fields and my Mennonite

grandmother never danced, never capered
or jitterbugged, didn't waltz one step in her life.
Stars pop like nipples on a nursing cow
as we walk out into the corn and sway among
the snakes and foxes, blind to the dance

of windmills churning the blameless black.

Roar

You become a clumsy lip-reader,
tease syllables,
watch them drown in dammed canals.
Shame of not knowing when to laugh.

These weeks when the world withdraws.
Your tormentors do not repeat loudly enough.
You are sick with asking.
Enter the clearing.

Ears gasp, exhale.
The winds of winter hiss through.
You are soaring, soaring
on the roar of the world.

Amnion

The roar of the world:
released rotary dial
spinning back to origin.

On the farm they shared
one line between four families.
No rule fierce enough to keep him
from lifting the wrong ring.

His world became a squall
of gossip. Seventy years and still
he bellows into receivers.

He is yelling now, wailing
into amniotic time—
each age a bubble
in the solvent of forever.

Each moment a sashay of the spoon,
every thought a proof
that every thing is soluble

Our lives voices, bleeding
under water. What's more lovely
than the way we sounded?
Static hiss and radio hush,

white noise and grey matter,
flare of final calcium wave—
waning, whispering, vanished.

The Ridge

How much dumb trust is left up here
in the clutch of swarming white?
Vast gape and the shuddering slough—
you dream yourself tumbling, tumbling.
He's not a cautious man, your guide.
Pretty basic, he grins. Don't fall.

Your task: forget the toll a fall
exacts in the stratospheric here.
Recall that you are not the guide—
perching on the edge of the white
slab of cornice, breaking tumbling
shards off the brink of sight. The slough's

hiss below. Naught but wind and slough.
A gasp and then the guide's whooped fall.
He drops over the ridge, tumbling
into familiar abyss. Here:
alone in whirl of darkling white.
Shrill howl, bright wind, Not dead, the guide

calls from the far-below. The guide
shouts, Just don't get caught in the slough,
and you are thinking of her white
toes, brushing off the covers. Fall
in this place and what you've brought here—
coupons and long johns and your tumbledown

life—this soaring now, that tumbled
then. Blurring layers and no guide
but gravity. Two paths from here:
over the rock, into the slough.
You look towards the absurd fall
line, tilting, pushing off the white

slant. Nothing now but a heartless white
slide between turn and tumble.
Watch the cliff's cragged knuckles fall
to its hips. And the baffled guide
waving and the gathering slough
and where to submit if not here?

Through the white haze you and your guide
tumble, together, caught in slough
that makes falling groundless, less here.

Wheel

This wheel of ours that turns the sky.
A withered wish, a vestibule.
This home becomes a spinning tomb.
Cells multiply. Astonishing.

A withered wish, a vestibule:
This wheeling hive of waning bright.
Cells multiply. Astonish me,
new flowers of forever-dark.

This wheeling hive of bygone bright,
penumbra of an alibi,
new flowers of forever-dark,
the final fishtail licks the sea.

When telescopes gored out our eyes,
this home became a spinning tomb.
Ill fit for death, we whirled and wept
this wheel of ours that turns the sky.

Star Digging

The stars buried in the backyard,
bridges spun from helium looms,
the sidereal hunger of worms.

You hatched seedlings from your beard,
asked what it would mean to exhume
the stars buried in the backyard.

Calculations coaxing dreams,
time gobbed in a cambered spoon's
sidereal hunger for worms.

Come morning trees begin to grow,
a blubber-milk aurora bloom
of stars buried in the backyard.

How to reflect that lightning dance,
how distill those latticework moons, reckon what
sidereal hunger forewarns.

The story is the one that always was
so of course it was you—you were
the stars buried in the backyard,
the real side of hungering worms.

Spool

Wildfire licking timber, munching pickups, prowling prairies,
men firing rivers through Super Soakers.

Twitter frozen, Facebook gone red, the southern hemisphere
feet deep how much sunscreen will it take.

Remember Newfoundland? Remember frogs? Remember
tossing the line out over and over,

getting nothing but rock cod they looked so dreadful
Jurassic you couldn't touch but

Grandpa threw them back in the river each time and it didn't
matter because what you really liked

    was reeling and reeling and reeling then letting the line unspool

AC-World

The bank teller said it was too cold,
but we would have followed the AC anywhere—
cinemas, libraries, fast food restaurants.

Entire days sacrificed to the gods
of Masonville Mall. Watching teens flirt
through astral frozen yogurt clouds.

Imagine a world before AC. Worse, afterwards:
the last stick of deodorant gone
and you, stuck in traffic on the 401.

No choice, now, but to make love
in the gum-shoe heat, turning your nose
from the waft of the planet's armpit.

Rectangle Glow

A galaxy of fingers, sweeping through the steep.
Our brains Sega jellyfish: squeeze, squeeze, sag.
And the bearded nuns grinning phosphor blue,
and the Mennonites munching Pringles,
and the oil-patch princess, omega lemon naiad,
face a million likes, dozing on a blimp of tattooed biceps.

Sleep plugged into steroids. Be gentle, I.V.
Be sweet. Eye muscles swollen with water weight.
An ocean of devices. Gazes kick in the undertow.
Grown men wear waterwings, crawl drained pools.
Our dreams rabbit ears, floppy disks, cassette tapes,
or else we do not dream.

Grate: Queen and Richmond

Face a Christmas of marquee light,
you stood on transplant streets, watched
grated steam rising eerie, rising slow.

Followed that shudder-still tornado
into the secret city's depths: engines boring
where you dove weightless, dove low

through granite chasms, through vapour
wastelands. You saw stalagmites weeping,
saw black tears oozing wearily below.

A child among the drilling minions
raised a hand—one finger, one thumb,
three stumps churning the underglow.

The child became a man, holding out
that hand for change and you went slack,
dreamsick, heard yourself muttering *no.*

You walked away thumbing change—
what change could sack a secret city, turn fingers
into lizard tails, help coral labyrinths grow?

Like stitches melting into wounds you saw
the bridges and the dams dissolve, watched
concrete wilt, rode the rivers' rage and flow.

Oil Weather

"We live the trope 'oil weather,' which was coined by early twentieth-century oil workers to describe the persistent fires so common to oil fields that they became naturalized as climate."

—Stephanie LeMenager

Picture Seam

"Picture a swamp. A hot, steamy, bug-infested, salt-water, tropical swamp ... Now picture this swamp in southwestern Ontario ... It is in this swamp where dying plant and animal life will fall, be covered in muck, and eventually, mysteriously, turned into a dark, thick substance that will someday make our society run the way it does."

—Gary May

I. Picture Tree

Picture a tree climbing out of a well:
yearn sumac, hush willow, cant sycamore,
watch maples stroke bedroom windows.

There is a rumour: when they brought
in the jerker lines, speculators kept sheep
in the fields to trim grass between rigs.

Picture a cauldron made of trees,
watch lightning shred its guts,
bore the belly of the vat, loose an ocean

of pitch to ignite the fields for a month
or more. The sniffer crabwalks
the snow-rugged north wood,

dowsing rod in mouth, hawthorn berries
tossed crimson in the fluff.
He scents cold earth, announces:

Picture the tale of a lizard, a tree
of tombs and rumours, hewn and wrought
into the road teamsters rode from Petrolia.

Does he wear a bearskin cloak?
Does he laugh with his mouth closed?
Did he hear the nitro shudder, watch the conspiracy

alight? Witness a man slither into a well,
a man made of mirrors, eyes peeled
lidless, drunk on churning unseen:
picture a sea climbing out of a stream.

II. Picture Sea

Picture a sea climbing out of a seam:
coven of polyps, sneering xiphactinus,
anemones luffing the silken reef.

In the beginning, a dank thatch of willow
roaring with mosquitoes. No lumber,
no mill. Swamp, sugar bush, swamp.

Picture seas gushing through colanders.
Picture whales made of mirrors, drifting
cankered caverns, roofs molared with salt.

Mosquitoes buzzed "uninhabitable" until
guides took settlers to stand hip-deep in pitch.
Plot by plot: sugar bush, then swamp.

The theory is rot. The theory is everything
decomposes and there is making in decay.
The theory is a coyote with human hands.

Drillers sank their boots in the bones
of the reef, brows smeared black against the bugs.
Currents whispered, "shale, limestone, shale."

Black ash stripped, hewn, gutted. Giants turned
three-pole derrick, wigwam mockery,
tree-bone forests blooming wasted fields.

When lightning bit the still its iron belly
gaped, sent viscera hissing over the fields.
No hook and ladder company, rainwater

selling for a dollar a barrel so the oil burned
for a month, lit the skirts of the sky
while jerker lines mourned and moaned.

The wells all parched, now, save for a dribble.
Each spring the creek floods its banks. In the
reservoir, salt crystals yearn for a gasp of sunlight,
picture a gash in the gut of the world.

III. Picture Gash

Picture a gush in the gut of the world
while the driller leaps and stomps a treadle,
springpole woodpeckering shale.

"If you wanted to bury Jimmy Hoffa,"
the descendent says, opening the tank,
"no one would ever find him here."

Twenty-five thousand barrels a day,
how could they have known the flood
would come rank and black?

He has built a replicant empire of oil.
"Do I wonder what it's like down there?"
He chin-jabs the earth. "Sure, we all do."

No ark so they made black ash muckpoles,
vaulted between stumps. Staunched the flow
when a driller suggested flax and catskin.

A driller stumbling among the creaking lines
at night, knowing the danger of kerosene
but still tossing light on that mouth.

Museums, fossils, fools. There are stories,
he explains, of a crude angel, a man
who'd drooled pitch, phoenixed over the fields.

A hundred feet, two. Shale, limestone, shale,
Shaw's black beard turning torch as he peers
through a seam in an ocean of stone,
pictures a gush in the glut of the world.

Periodic Ode: Sodium

You howl through my blood like antelope thunderstorms.
The gentle years have made you dearer than nicotine.
You thrill my arteries, charm the snakes of taste.
Your tickle turns my tongue to purr.
No care for executive chefs, no tips for waiters who try
to shame, I beg and plead and table-thump for you.

How you saturate the seas of me. How you helped
mariners tack the belligerent Atlantic. How you sparred
Newfoundland winters, coating the cod
that chewed the gums of every toothless bride.
Uneasy solace: when the carrion descend the waves of salt
and water I call self will dissolve, take flight, soar.

Periodic Ode: Oxygen

The Moth said I could not live
or die without you. Bono said
with or without you, oh no.
The curious thing is I can live,
live as the world throws doughnuts,
turn radius shrinking prolific,

friends and followers, bookmarks and scars.
Nothing seems to never get smaller.
But you. The baffling thing is I can live
with the forests sprinting for mountain tops,
live with fronds breaching Antarctica,
live with belligerent fungus thriving
and powerflowers seeping,

live with all I love in jeopardy—
but I cannot breathe without you.
I am an infant forever crawling
down stairs for the first time.
Hold a breath and consider.
Where have you been, lungful?
What secrets long forgotten?
What worlding words have formed
and vanished in the hush of your anima?

Periodic Ode: Carbon

Remember the good times
we had during the apocalypse?

The excitement of watching

continents flood and starve?
Remember the second

coming of the dinosaurs?
Or that species of

genetically modified
peacocks, the ones with tails

made out of sunsets?
Ah, the radiance of rapture,

the poultice of ozone—
magnificent stench
of a thermophilic orb.

Chemical Valley

while listening to Ashbery's Flow Chart

The berries had grown black and sweet and ripe
and poison snakes were writhing in the shrubs so you
had to be careful where you placed your feet.
The trucks were climbing up and up the bridge to the USA
green energy trucks and Wonderbread trucks
and the President's Choice trucks climbing up
before tumbling out the open mouth and into the river's
unimpeachable blue. The water a brilliant, brilliant blue
but the ratio was off. The ratio of male to female was all wrong
and there weren't enough male starlings, weren't enough
male seagulls, weren't enough male cardinals and imagine
a world without those livid red gusts of wonder in the armpits of trees.
The rumours of asphalt sprouted highways through the sky,
lightning fossilized in a concrete beach.

Herd

The two-legged horses do not roam the field
oldest instinct to fly do not stray the field
because thirst, horsepowerless thirst choiceless thirst
ordaining: dip and rise ride hot thirsty fields, sway
narcotic for passersby in parched rabid fields
where no horse can fly narcotic over open grassland
over the counterweight the walking beam
beside the walking beam the bridle beneath that
Samson post and deep the reservoir hence the horses
pinned over the reservoir horses nodding swaying
for a taste hence the lack of running
tastes like fingertip smear coal black jet black
equine lips one way crude the other gas
nod-bobbing crude bedtime rhythm
horseheads glugging not pattering nothing to suggest
this glug-glugging rhythm might stop when the last Operator
hoses horses, mishears whispers of thirst.

Petrolia, 1867

Bootprints in mud
muckers pole-vaulting log to log
scuzzed fingernails clawing
lips of earth
pandemonium of three-pole derricks
Shaw stomping on springboard stomping
until gusher roars into sky
black scar gashing the blue
sulphurous crude hurricane splatting fields
lathering fields and the creeks choking the creeks
steam engines jerker lines a thousand iron horse heads
nodding donkeys fucking
down through shale and shale blasting
nitro dangling in tin cans
lightning striking thousand-barrel still
fire burning for two weeks
bear creek black creek clogged with crude
men named Fairbank or Vaughn
opening banks, raising hotels and calling them "Iroquois"
men named Fairbank or Vaughn building stills
and the word "refine" a leech on their tongues
black leech suckling on the teat of their tongues
in Charlottetown English men and French men
wear tailcoats light cigars eat lobster
men named Tupper Cartier MacDonald
men unable to decipher their dreams—
a nation built on a porous reservoir
ancient underworld hungering
to burn into gas and ride the sky
a sea of spirits bellowing *petrol patrol parole.*

Gush

Let's go back and look at that 90 foot gusher,
an important contribution to Canada's economy
which would eventually be translated into a better life for all.

Canada is an oil-hungry nation geared to an oil economy.
Crude oil discovery at Leduc was a dramatic and exciting thing.
Let's go back and look at that 90 foot gusher:

There was no gusher—only a flow to the flare
several hundred yards from the well,
which would eventually be translated into a better life for all.

As an example of the misunderstanding we suffered
(the impression that we had struck an immense flow of oil),
let's go back and look at that 90 foot gusher.

Mike Turts, the farmer who owned the land
on which the well was located,
believed other wells soon would be drilled in the area,
which would eventually be translated into a better life for all.

He is of foreign extraction and speaks broken English
(our greatest overall danger: those not owning
mineral rights beneath their land).
Let's go back and look at that 90 foot gusher
which would eventually be translated into a better life for all.

Colloquium: J.T. Henry and Lady Simcoe on Early Ontario Petrocolonialism

Mrs. Hamilton drank tea with me. Mrs. McGill, wife of the commissary,
Capt. John McGill, and Miss Crookshank, her sister,
are pleasant women from New York. I gave a dance this evening.

The oil springs on Oil Creek formed a part
of the religious ceremony of the Seneca Indians,
who formerly lived on these wild hills.

The Governor set off from hence in a sleigh,
with six officers and twenty soldiers.
Brant and twenty Indians are to join him and guide him.

A spring of real petroleum was discovered on the march
by its offensive smell. The Aborigines dipped it from their wells
and mixed it with their war-paint,
which is said to have given them a hideous appearance.

The governor found his expectations perfectly realized
as to the goodness of the country on the banks of La Tranche,
and is confirmed in his opinion that the fork of the river
is the most proper site for the capital of the country,
to be called New London.

The "thick scum" which the Indians gathered,
and which careful, prudent men, now guard against conflagration,
flows into peaceable tanks, and, instead of lighting up the wilderness
for uncouth savages, sends joy and comfort
into thousands of distant homes.

I have been very much amused by reading Watson on chemistry,
in which there is an account of the making of an artificial volcano
that I think would please you.

The thought is quite romantic—perhaps poetic—
that the little animals which occupied these shells
ages before men appeared
allowed their substance to be converted into oil to fill them,
and thus, with true charity, even "gave their bodies to be burned."

We dined with Mrs. Hamilton, wife of Mr. Robert Hamilton, and
struck a vein of gas and oil which spouted over the top of the derrick,
and was fired by the night lamp hung
in the derrick, burning the rigging down.

I observed some trees on fire; the flames,
in part concealed, appeared like stars
the odor of the oil is rather unpleasant
and the music would sound well among the rocks.

Phonemevolution

Vanishing Sestina

Back then we were still fucking like [a].
This was pre-disease. We chopped lines, shot [b]
in barrels. We didn't know the [c]
yet, that wound in the clouds, crown of the [d].
What did we know? We knew our futures [e]
wither, knew the scorpions on [f]

tiles were twitching, skittering, knew "[f]"
was euphemism for toilet. [a]
sprinting in front of our headlights [e]
haunt us through the night. There were no more [b]
in the lake so our dogs mounted the [d]
and humped wild, our tame castrated [c]

lives looked brilliant from space or the [c]
was a snarling ruse. What undreamt [f]
antics are left when the blunt open [d]
was torn and weeping, the timid [a]
quaking in disbelief because no [b]
nor predators remain. What wounds [e]

bloom through the whisper-murk? Astral tears [e]
dripping through emptiness, soundless [c]
fathoms of space with no water, no [b],
no tentacles tell me where's the [f]?
All your life has been afterthought. [a]
fucking like humans fucking like apes, [d]

is a carpet where planes drag their tails. [d]
smears the minds of pointing toddlers who [e]
built a waterfront of diapers. [a]
on fire, darting through dark fields the [c]
no longer protects from the Last [f]
Incident, the curious rage of [b],

the strange silent fury of plastic [b]
floating through bathtub memories, the [d]
lingering since you looked out the [f]
window and saw it fractured, leaking. [e]
you had known tears of light were just [c]
drip you could have spared the sickly [a].

If there's a place where the rugged [b][e]
still, then there are still [f]aces [c]rafting,
gnawing [a] labyrinth of [c]ash.

Thirteen Ways of Hearing "Thirteen Ways of Looking at a Blackbird"

Thirteen ways of looking at a fracture
Thirteen days of looking at The Rapture
Thirteen braised doves hooking a la raptor
Thirteen blazed up wookies and a tractor
Thirteen tasers zooking rats at Blackburn
Thirteen daisies looking sad at practise
Thirteen aged loves, booked in ads and captured
Worst keen plays that took in starving actors:
Burt, Weened Days, Loved Books, Inked Dada, Jack's Turn
Burst spleens, glazed (a cooking fad at Halpern)
Curt Ian's way was brooking Grandma's laughter
Burnt teens lazed—gloves shook, ink ran, and after:
Thirteen ways of looking at a trapped world

Rapunzel's Rapt Uncle

"Rapunzel Rapunzel, let down your hair"
"Rapunzel Rapunzel, get down from there"
"Rapunzel Rapunzel, less frown more flare!"
Rapunzel's rapt uncle, vest brown and fair
Avuncular fundler, stepped round her snares
Crept under the bungalow, besting a hare
Rapunzel rapped fungal, pets sounded rare
Rapunzel dread-trundled, fled down the stairs
Rap's uncle grabbed under-dress, found her bare
Rapunzel's rad ungulate leapt round the chairs
Grabbed thunder, trapped uncle, fed Brown (her bear)
Rapunzel's rapt uncle was downed over there
Rapunzel wrapped bundles (flesh ground for fare)
Craft'd thumbfulls of uncle, nest-crowned her hair

The Dead Feel Narrow

Though such dear friends
had gone

the dead feel
narrow

days in vain
wander

seaside the blight
thickens

Vile Heights, Vile Heights!

Vile heights, vile heights—
purr violently?
Vile heights, stood treed,
hours clutched fur free.

Brute bile's chagrin,
tuna scarfed in sport.
Run swifter, dunces,
run swifter, art.

Roaming in freedom,
dog got me.
Frights I've endured on nights
in trees.

Don It, Gloried Lord

Britain wins the orchard, ass-whips Verdun's thin muskets!

Crest high, balloon! Shoot ardourless love! Ride
wild rough clouds against oxish hour! Confine
disease known for shit-smelling scourge, come line
up orgies drinking-bands would fine.
                                                            Seaside:
A child-smashed rhizome drummed up yesterdays.
Eyes refused window-crumbs where leavings led.
Fears won where jazzy tunes—deaf spillage, bled—
handbraked the sirens.
                                        Sad baths lave the aging
belle. Sand's seeded wrinkles shone before,
though fair ones brightened into creeping days.

What rains drew men that distant daughters gave?
Pray! Fear! A war in elephants galore—
vile triumph blooms bile. Fife's song tore up debt's
new blaze. Which enemy won fair doomsday's test?

Evander's Wheels

Evander peals through Mexico,
a dreamy rose-kissed Romeo.
A scarred embrace, an infant's cry,
a nark, Bill, lamely zings on by.
Fierce lure: *I need a fish taco.*

Where is that bread? What brays that goat?
She weaved along the undertow.
Shove after shove rent sour her cry:
"Evander feels!"

Break up that coral, fish for toes.
Say! Brew some baby hands for show.
Ha! Scorch neighbours who scold the shy.
Iffy; grey rape will rust through lies.
He falls asleep, jalopies blow,
Evander reels.

Tough Tea

Dark cupless tea—man's darling bliss—
bow brittle, hats tipped, now dim eyes deceive with
Brits' cupped tea. First man vowed—"Fuck tea!"—
then finest tea howled true love's rimmèd glee.
Now Moses spat his bannocky bread,
asking, "For shame! Sports tossed-off schadenfreude?"
Headless envoys ignored this brew then sampled
Delphic troves, won dud days of lieutenants' gall-sass,
hissed: "Morgan, tea! Good brew!"

*

Allay, free wives in Dundee fair,
(fairly honest, save Nora's buried scar:
brisk tea with two men, sly rank kiss,
soured carriages, then barraged tempered bliss).
Slow barons judging droolers' pets
(embroidered things we've given all to get).
Sloe juice may queue rapture till tea,
lest doffed new hats shelve surer habits:
reason's sacrilege, needs unfilled in tea.

*

Fool landlubbers at bow rinsed
poor old Brinewhale in tubs of innards.
When warring, blood's whiskey filled the sea,
legs kept intact, chopped snitches' tough lumpy
necks howled *Triumph!* Damned days' fat sour
rinds rot while shelved stores ween the meagre crow.
Lips blue, spent, spurned now. Salt tears, teacupped.
Stomachs squander, retch prowled meals. Beautiful
taste, mast-gripped tea—death's hooked, fife-drum sea.

Phonemevolution

Your alkaline purr, your sciency light,
the way you make my eyes burn.

Poor aquiline churl, Her Highness sleeps tight,
she razed two snakes by wives' urns.

Ural can fine Burrel, score giant freak lice,
debate whose quakes whined wilder.

Sure, Oppenheim Earls, Porsche clients breed mice,
sedate blue whales drive Chryslers.

Pure Talcum-fine worlds, poured ions leak bright.
Today new waves made dyes blur.

Learned falcons eye squirrels, gird lions, alight.
To wade through lakes, vile thighs churn.

Her Delta-wine slur, porn financed these flights
(two males to 'bate mile-high worms).

Pervs' alcky-lined sperm, furred blinds seemed right.
Rum-jailed, toothache defied Vern.

For salt and lime girls, horned giants leave bites,
delayed poos slake Mai Tai squirm.

Lure Malta-mined pearls for scion-sweet nights,
Tuesdays you shake while I stir.

Tour awkward-lined words (torn silence bleeds nice),
Hooray! Debased bright lies turn.

Phylogeny

"a title is never finished; it is only abandoned"

—misquotation of W.H. Auden paraphrasing Paul Valéry

i.

Paradise Glossed
Paradise Tossed
Paradise Embossed
Paradise Double-Crossed
Paradise Lost and Found
Paradise II: The Dashboard Light
Paradise Walking In Memphis
Paradise Lust
Paradise Chuffed
Paradise Rebuffed
Pair of Dice, Tossed

ii.

What We Talk About When We Talk About Fuzz
What We Talk About When We Talk About Duds
What We Talk About When We Talk About Mild Winters
What We Talk About When We Rock Sold Out Clubs
What We Talk About When We're Withholding
Killer Stories About Ourselves
What We Talk About When We Talk About Duck Face
What We Talk About When We Talk About *Making a Murderer*
What We Talk About When We Talk About
James Franco's Course at NYU
What We Talk About When We Talk About Toxic, Festering Envy
What We Talk About When We Talk About Raymond Carver
What We Talk About When We Talk About
Aggressive Minimalism and Hard-Luck Wisdom
What We Talk About When We Talk About The New Sincerity
What We Talk About When We Talk About
Big Hearts Through Tiny Key Holes
What We Talk About When We Talk About Earning Your Epiphanies
What We Talk About When We Talk About
Alcoholism and Proletarian Angst
What We Talk About When We Talk About The Anxiety of Influence
What We Talk About When We Box Without Gloves

iii.

Civilization and Its Impotence
Civilization and Its Increments
Civilization and Inadequate Vents
Civilization Incontinence
Civilization and Its Discotheques
Civilization and Increasing Rent
Civilization and Its Distinct Scents
Civilization and Its Discus Events
Civilization's Angry Distant Parents
Civilization and Its Circus Tents
Civilized Nations and Itemized Dissent
Civil Migrations and Itinerants
Civil Vibrations in Convents

iv.

Gore and Peace
Mangled Karenina
Do Androids Scheme in a Restless Sleep?
The Old Man and the Seizure
The Bun Also Rises
The Sun Also Rides Us
The Gun: Also Size-ist
The Nun Also Metastasizes
Fear and Loathing in Bodegas
Fear and Loathing in Tornados
Fear and Loathing in Krakatoa
A Tale of Two Pretty
White Boys
Rad Behaviour
Batch 22
Grave New World
Chores and *Grease*
Beer and Trembling
Of Mice and Manopause
Sir Gawain and the Dream Flight
Irate Gatsby
Beyond the Severed Principal
What We Talk About When We Talk About Civilizations
Dreaming Lost Paradises of Discontent

Jellegiac

immersed in Gwen Hovey's "Jelly"

I. Subjarine

The jar, like the creatures, was lucent,
otherwise you would not have seen:

dull bar-light, puffed features, love's loose skin,
otherwise you would not have been

a darling, a teacher's buzzed nuisance,
lovers' cries you would not redeem.

Babr's night-raw detours galumphing,
otherwise you would not have gleaned

a scarlet where sea-tears scuzzed, drooping—
blubber-wise your world caught, careened.

What scarred thing rubbed deeper, dug tooth in,
smothered lives you should not have dreamed?

II. A Jar Ajar, or, What if the Jar Wore a J-Cloth Bonnet and Served Coffee in a 1950's Diner?

Slender tentacle, tender ventricle,
the men you've penned with rented will.
You see there was a crack in the ocean.

Tend your till, wend your tented frill,
then lend true blends (indentured swill).
There was seawater seeping through the aperture.

Menders will hem where dentists drill,
defend bruised land, fix bent ids' ill.
A fracture, leaking poison, and we had to live our daily lives.

Blenders still rend pure hens, wet krill.
Women stoop end over end, until:
being boneless, the Medusozoa passes the slightest seam.

III. Jellegy

I have seen death beating like a gelatine
heart on the sun-howled strand.
All the gum that ever tongued up from sidewalks
wobbled in a single liquid eye.
Maybe colour is a measure
of time, your chromic pandemonium the work
of a hundred million years, all of it
undone as you drawl lucent on the beach.

I played *Super Mario* once, dodged the lovely glitching bobs of you.
Twenty-five years later you passed floating as I swam against the tide.
You opened and hushed like a lily, a whispering sphincter.
The seal's slick head glistened thirty feet away.

Back on the beach you slurred blisterish in the sun and I heard
death bleating like a gelatine heart on the sun-howled strand.
I raised a twig and prodded the raw yolkless egg of you.
I longed for you to feel pain, yearned
to dwell with you in a Kuroshio of hurt.

Strange monomania: empathy tunes
ego's fangs, sweetens the suck of self-drawn blood,
yet many nights I still hear you wheezing
liquid through bathymetries of dream.

Notes

"Scorpions" is a sonnenizio beginning with a line from Shakespeare's *Macbeth.* "Cosmic Follicles" is a modified sonnenizio beginning with a line from "Jeepster" by T. Rex. I was introduced to the sonnenizio through the work of John Barton.

"Trichotillomaniac Reports from Periscope Depth" is a glosa that recycles lines from T.S. Eliot's "Mr. Apollinax."

"Mutants' Songnet" is inspired by Catriona Wright's poem "Date Night #2."

All text in "Gush" has been mined from an Imperial Oil document entitled "Public relations aspects of the Leduc oil discovery. – February, 1948." This document is available online through the Imperial Oil Archives, housed at Calgary's Glenbow Museum (IOLpub-1a-3).

"Colloquium" is a pilfered erasure dialogue extracted from fragments of two public domain texts: J.T. Henry's *The Early and Later History of Petroleum* (1873) and *The Diary of Mrs. John Graves Simcoe, Wife of the Lieutenant Governor of Upper Canada 1792-6* (1911). Italicized lines come from Lady Simcoe's diary, unitalicized lines from Henry's *History of Petroleum.*

The following poems are full mondegreens of original sources (listed in parentheses):

"The Dead Feel Narrow"
("The Red Wheel Barrow"—William Carlos Williams)

"Vile Heights, Vile Heights!"
("Wild Nights, Wild Nights"—Emily Dickinson)

"Don It, Gloried Lord"
(Sonnet #44 [from *Elegiac Sonnets*]—Charlotte Smith)

"Evander's Wheels"
("In Flanders Fields"—John McCrae)

"Tough Tea"
("The Flea"—John Donne)

The full mondegreen is a form invented by Andy Verboom and based on the misheard lyric ("the girl with kaleidoscope eyes" → "the girl with colitis goes by"). Sylvia Wright coins the term "mondegreen" and signals its poetic potential in her lovely 1954 essay, "The Death of Lady Mondegreen." Full mondegreens map (more or less) phoneme by phoneme onto the sonic structure of original poems to create phonetic underworlds. For more on the form, see the chapbook *Full Mondegreens*, co-authored by myself and Andy Verboom (Frog Hollow 2016). In addition to the full mondegreens listed above, the poems "Phonemevolution," "Songnet," and "A Phylogeny of Titles" also riff on the mondegreen form.

Acknowledgements

These pilfered, borrowed, recycled, regurgitated, and repurposed words were written on the ancestral lands of the Anishinaabek, Haudenosaunee, Lūnaapéewak, Attawandaron, and Mi'kmaq. The active treaties are the London Township and Sombra Treaties of 1796, the Dish with One Spoon Covenant Wampum, and the Peace and Friendship Treaties. I acknowledge and thank the people, the animals, the plants, the water, and the living land.

The idea of the "humanimalchine," lifted from Dominic Pettman, is the animating animus of this book.

Huge thanks to my editor, Jim Johnstone. Thank you for your eye and ear, for believing in this experiment and testing it. Thanks also to Aimée Parent Dunn and the rest of the fine folks at Palimpsest Press.

Previous incarnations of poems from this collection have appeared in *The Walrus*, *Grain*, *Prairie Fire*, *EVENT*, *Contemporary Verse 2*, *PRISM international*, *Hart House Review*, *The Puritan*, *carte blanche*, *The Dalhousie Review*, and *The Antigonish Review*. Thanks to the editors, staff, and volunteers at those magazines.

"Colloquium: J.T. Henry and Lady Simcoe on Early Ontario Petrocolonialism" won *The Walrus*' 2016 Poetry Prize.

Several of the poems in "Phonemevolution" were previously published in *Full Mondegreens*, a chapbook co-authored by myself and Andy Verboom. *Full Mondegreens* was co-winner of Frog Hollow Press' 2016 chapbook contest. Andy is a champion.

Thanks to my family, my parents, my friends, and the robust literary communities in London and Halifax. Thanks to Natasha for time and space, feedback and patience. To Rose and Sybille for bending my world. Particular thanks to those who bent their ears and minds to this work in its gestation: Andy Verboom, Tom Cull, Madeline Bassnett, Blair Trewartha, Kevin Shaw, David W. Janzen, Jason Sunder, Riley MacDonald, David White, Christine Thorpe, Peggy Roffey, Ola Nowosad, Aaron Kreuter.

About the Author

David Huebert has won *The Walrus* Poetry Prize, the CBC Short Story Prize, and has twice been a Nominee for the National Magazine Awards. David's fiction debut, *Peninsula Sinking*, won the Jim Connors Dartmouth Book Award, was shortlisted for the Alistair MacLeod Short Fiction Prize, and was runner-up for the Danuta Gleed Literary Award. David's poems have been published in magazines such as *Prairie Fire*, *Event*, and *The Walrus*. His poetry chapbook, *Full Mondegreens* (with Andy Verboom) won the Frog Hollow Chapbook contest in 2016. He lives, writes, and teaches in K'jipuktuk/Halifax.